TIERRA Y LIBERTAD

PHOTOGRAPHS
OF MEXICO 1900-1935
FROM THE
CASASOLA ARCHIVE

MUSEUM OF MODERN ART OXFORD

Preparation, Research and Education

in the Fototeca of the National Institute of
Anthropology and History by:
Servando Arechiga
Marco Antonio Hernandex Badillo
Edith Durana Calva
Flora Lara Klahr
Aurora Martinez
Gilda Noguerola
Rolando Fuentes Sanchez
Alejandra del Valle
in the Museum of Modern Art, Oxford, by:
Paul Bonaventura
Carol Brown
Graham Halstead
Toby Jackson
Franta Provaznik

Opposite page:
**Emiliano Zapata, leader of the Revolution in
the south. c. 1912**

ISBN 0 905836 51 0
Published 1985 by the Museum of Modern Art,
Oxford, to accompany the exhibition *Tierra y
Libertad: Photographs of Mexico 1900-1935 from
the Casasola Archive*, 16 June to 28 July 1985
© Museum of Modern Art, Oxford, and the
Instituto Nacional de Antropologia
y Historia, Mexico
Exhibition selected by David Elliott for the
Museum of Modern Art, Oxford, and Eleazar
Zamora for the Fototeca, Pachuca (INAH)

Catalogue designed by David King
Translation by Pamela Francis
and Marco Livingstone
Sub-edited by Sarah Bourne
Printed by Shadowdean Ltd, London
Photoset by Lithoprint Ltd, London

A list of all Museum of Modern Art publications in
print can be obtained from the Bookshop
Manager at the Museum of Modern Art,
30 Pembroke Street, Oxford OX1 1BP.

This exhibition has been organised by the
Museum of Modern Art, Oxford, with the National
Institute of Anthropology and History and the
Cultural Department of the Ministry of Foreign
Affairs of the Government of Mexico. It has
received financial assistance from the Visiting
Arts Unit of Great Britain and Northern Ireland.
The Museum of Modern Art is subsidised by the
Arts Council of Great Britain.

"In those days nobody's secrets were safe from the camera." — Carlos Monsiváis

Foreword

This exhibition of one hundred and fifty prints has been selected from the many thousands of negatives which form the Casasola Archive. Its title, 'Tierra y Libertad', takes up the rallying call for 'Land and Liberty' which expressed the aspirations of the Mexican Revolution.

The opening of the exhibition coincides with two important events: the seventy-fifth anniversary of the beginning of the Mexican Revolution, and the visit of President Miguel de la Madrid to Great Britain.

Since the mid-1970s when the Casasola collection was acquired by the Mexican government, the Archive has been administered by the National Institute of Anthropology and History. It is housed in the former convent of San Francisco in Pachuca, the chief city of the state of Hidalgo, some eighty miles north-east of the capital. The Archive contains the work of many photographers (both Mexican and foreign) collected by Casasola, as well as the considerable number of photographs he took himself. The riches of this Archive are just beginning to be appreciated as old negatives are reprinted and new material discovered. This exhibition is little more than an introduction to what is a largely unknown and unparalleled collection of early documentary photography.

Mexico and its history may seem remote, complicated, even exotic. This selection of work is intended to break down the barriers erected by such images. Britain has had many links with Mexico and, appropriately, the city of Pachuca bears testimony to this history. The legacy of the nineteenth-century Cornish and Welsh miners who made it into a prosperous centre for silver and other precious ores can still be seen on the streets — the Victorian hotels with their English names, and the older houses. Even the pasties first brought by the Cornishmen, now made with chilli, are still very much a local delicacy. A more poignant memory remains in the now unused British cemetary, cupped in the hills behind the city.

We hope that this exhibition and others like it will help to re-establish and strengthen the links between our two countries. It is part of a continuing exploration of Mexican art and culture in which the Museum of Modern Art is engaged. In 1980 we had a major exhibition of the work of José Clemente Orozco; last summer we showed a retrospective of the photographs of Manuel Alvarez Bravo; in 1986 an exhibition on the Soviet film-maker Sergei Eisenstein will closely examine the three decisive years he spent working in Mexico. Subsequently we hope to present an exhibition on the relationship between Mexico and Surrealism which is now being researched in the University of Mexico. Future projects will undoubtedly develop.

Many people have worked to bring about this exhibition and I should like to thank them warmly for their commitment and help. In addition to those listed elsewhere, I should like to mention Dr Carlos Monsiváis, Dr Ida Rodriguez Prampolini, formerly Cultural Attaché at the Mexican Embassy in London, Barbara Litwin, Second Secretary in the Mexican Embassy, Helen Escobedo, Art Consultant for UNAM, Professor Alistair Hennessy of the University of Warwick, Michael Gonzalez of the University of Glasgow, Professor Peter Calvert of the University of Southampton, Ruskin College, Oxford, and the 1982 Theatre Company, who have all most kindly helped in the presentation of this exhibition and its related lectures.

David Elliott
Director
Museum of Modern Art, Oxford

Introduction

Agustín Víctor Casasola, the photographer of the first social revolution of the twentieth century, was also the founder of the first photographic archive in Mexico and a militant trade union activist. As a photographic reporter he worked for the political section of the newspaper 'El Tiempo' and also for 'El Imparcial', the most important daily of the time.

His intense activity as a reporter led him to join the Mexican Journalists' Association. Later, in 1911, he founded the Society of Press Photographers and, shortly afterwards, the Photographic Information Agency, the first of its kind in Mexico.

The Revolution which transformed Mexico brought about, among many other things, a national awareness. During those years every region of the country, convulsed by armed struggle and social conflict, established its true identity.

From these intense and terrible years there emerged before the Mexicans' own eyes a country of sharp contrasts — infinitely diverse, with changing geography and a thousand faces. One of the most acclaimed of Agustín Víctor Casasola's skills is that he knew how to depict his country. Another ability, perhaps his greatest, was his capacity to express sensitively and artistically the many faces of the men and women of Mexico as they struggled and lived through the Revolution.

To his fine artistic sensitivity Casasola brought an acute sense of history. In 1921, when the aftermath of war had not yet died away, Casasola decided to collect his work together in an 'Album histórico gráfico'. This, the first photographic chronicle of the Revolution, was the basis of the later and more famous 'Historia gráfica de la Revolución Mexicana' which so enriched later generations of Mexicans.

Casasola's work today forms the richest photographic testimony of the revolutionary armed struggle, of Mexico's social and political life, and of the role of the people in the building of contemporary Mexico. The Casasola Archive is, as well as an historical record and a work of art, an inexhaustible source of reference for researchers, writers and artists. Casasola's impressions of Mexico have now been rediscovered for their aesthetic merit. They are making Mexico known to the world.

Dr Enrique Florescano
Director General
National Institute of Anthropology and
History (INAH)

Boy soldier

Agustín Víctor Casasola: Photographer and Collector

'A photograph can be an exact impression of your words.' So read the text of an advertisement which the American Photo Supply Company had placed in 'El Imparcial', the most important daily of the last decade of the dictatorship of Porfirio Díaz. It was advertising film, paper, developing and printing equipment as well as such specialised monthly magazines as 'El fotógrafo mexicano', for professionals, and 'El arte de la fotografía' for amateurs. This was 1900, the dawn of the century. North America's and Europe's commercial production of dry gelatine plates and of roll film and plate cameras had expanded to take in markets in countries where industrial expansion was booming. In less than twenty years an enthusiastic interest in photography had developed as well as a popular demand, need and taste for its use. Everything could be questioned except the accuracy and truth of the picture produced by the camera.

Newspapers and magazines which thought of themselves as modern published not only photographic advertisements, but also notes and reports on the latest advances in photography. In the Sunday sections of 'El Imparcial' articles appeared from Mexican and foreign contributors on technical points ('Photographs without a lens. Surprising developments'; 'The photographic rifle'; 'Landscape photography'); on its application to war ('The use of telephotography in logistics'); on its use in medicine ('Radiography, a photographic proof of the illness you are suffering from'); and on its application in publicity. Even the advertisements provided basic information and heightened general awareness of the possibilities of photography.

The illustrated magazines organised photographic competitions — of child portraits, landscapes, townscapes and fashion — and exhibited the prize-winning pictures. In their illustrated editions, they printed pictures from the most prestigious studios, and publicised their work with eulogistic reports about the luxury of their fittings and equipment, the excellence of their portraits, and the careful skills of the photographers. In this way, the photographic and the information industries promoted each other. The Valleto brothers, Emilio Lange, Wolfstein, Photo Schlattman and O. de la Mora, amongst others, were the sanctified names of this new art; without their compliance the faces of high society were left out of the news. The same was true in the world of politics. The photographic industry consolidated the power of the image and made it a natural medium for the image of power. 'El Mundo Ilustrado', the weekly produced by 'El Imparcial', always opened with a political section which reported on the activities (not all, of course) of the cabinet of Porfirio Díaz. The other papers tried to do the same, although without the same resources. At that time, about 1900, the young journalist Agustín Víctor Casasola, reporter on 'El Tiempo', the Catholic newspaper of Mexico City, put aside his pen and began to devote himself to photography. He photographed the official activities of the Porfirio Díaz dictatorship and, less frequently, sport, fashion, news, culture and popular customs. Shortly afterwards, he was asked to contribute to 'El Imparcial' as well, and to other newspapers in the capital.

Between 1900 and 1910 — the last decade of the Díaz regime — Casasola acquired indispensable practical experience which would be fundamental to his future development. Working alongside such writers as José María Roa Bárcenas, Joaquín García Icazbalceta, José María Vigil, Andrés Molina Enríquez and Esquivel Obregón — contributors to 'El Tiempo' — awoke in him an interest in history and narrative. The task of news-gathering stirred a passion for documentary. The medium and environment in which he worked, the contacts he made, and his activities with the union (in 1903 he became a member of the Mexican Journalists' Association, a mutual benefit society) formed in him a clear perception of the function of a press photographer. During those ten productive years he developed a style which was not purely personal, but shared with other press photographers. It was marked by a common choice and treatment of subjects and viewpoints, it obeyed canons which the official press had already laid down — to give prominence to the image of the Establishment. The dictator, cabinet ministers, élite intellectuals and society families were all shown as the focus around which revolved any happening worthy of consideration. The life of the people was not completely disregarded but was included only as an element of contrast or social context.

Photography and cinema were the two new discoveries by those in power which, together with the press, served to promote their own favourable image. Consequently, the repertoire of images which were allowed was limited to shots of parties, processions, banquets, receptions, scenes showing the promotion and demotion of officials — all without any further requirement than that General Porfirio Díaz should appear decisively in the foreground. The conditions of life and work on ranches, in the mines and factories and on the land were taboo for the commercial press. The slightest infringement was paid for in the cells of the Belén Prison; here even Victoriano Agüeros, the owner of 'El Tiempo', was forced to spend time more than once.

By the time of the first blasts of revolution, Casasola was thirty-five years old and established in his profession. Slowly and cautiously, he began to report on Madero's campaign against Díaz. But like all the other reporters he preferred to centre attention on the last show of the Díaz dictatorship: the celebrations of the first centenary of independence, with which the government tried, through the press, to hide its political crisis. By focusing on these festivities, the press strove to present the image of a strong government. However, even at that time in the centre and north of the country preparations were being made for the armed uprising which was to break out a few weeks later— in November 1910. In May 1911 the insubordination of Generals Francisco (Pancho) Villa and Pascual Orozco against the orders of Madero, their leader, led to the first revolutionary victory, the taking of Ciudad Juárez. The aristocratic ultra-Catholic, Francisco Leon de la Barra, became acting President while elections were called.

At that time, Agustín Casasola founded the Society of Press Photographers, made up of fifteen reporters, amongst whom were his brother Miguel and H. J. Gutiérrez. One of the most outstanding acts of the society was to interview the acting President, thanking him for his kindness and courtesy, and offering their congratulations because 'You have inaugurated the era of liberty for press photography'. There is little to indicate, however, that either Casasola or his colleagues had ever been harassed by the Díaz government, for which they had worked so enthusiastically.

In December 1911, as soon as Francisco I. Madero had taken over the presidency, Casasola invited him to a photographic exhibition he had organised which showed the work of the members of the Photographers' Society. The central motif was the Anti-Re-electionist movement and the armed struggle headed by Madero. From that time onwards Casasola showed a singular capacity to adapt himself to political changes at the same speed as they took place.

Political events continued to rage: Félix Díaz, Pascual Orozco, Flores Magón and Zapata rose against Madero's government, although for different reasons. Their political conflicts and differences were reflected in the press, supporting one or the other side. These events led to the disappearance of some newspapers and the creation of others, as well as to the dissolution of the Society of Press Photographers. 'El Tiempo' stopped its presses in 1912; in 1914, when the Constitutionalists triumphed, 'El Imparcial' was also closed down. As the old regime disappeared, so did the press for which Casasola had worked. Now, in the midst of the Revolution, with his initiative and great capacity for work — well known for his experience and collection of photographs — and above all with his characteristic commercial sense, Casasola decided to set up, with his friend Gonzalo Herrerías, the Photographic Information Agency, the first of its kind in Mexico. He was careful to keep a prudent distance from any political position. He began to work as an independent photographer, supplying pictures to national and foreign newspapers of different tendencies. Shortly afterwards Gonzalo Herrerías was offered the editorship of a newspaper. Casasola decided to remain in charge of the business, together with his brother Miguel and his young son Gustavo — who was later to be the editor of the Archive — as well as his staff of photographers. These had been employed to cover various events in Mexico City and, occasionally, to travel in regions where the revolutionary armies advanced victoriously against the federal strongholds.

The period of the civil war was one of intensive work for Casasola, but official functions continued to be his usual field of interest: cabinet members, interviews, civic celebrations, diplomatic receptions, political tours. Although the Casasolas themselves were quick to promote the legend, Agustín was not the 'photographer of the Revolution' in the sense of recording the military confrontations in the field. He continued to provide illustrations for news bulletins in the capital, as in his previous work for 'El Tiempo' and 'El Imparcial'. As a result there are only a few original pictures of the Revolution in the Archive, and, of those that exist, most are by other photographers. Casasola was fundamentally an urban photographer. The best of his work — and that produced by his colleagues — informs on aspects of the social scene in Mexico City.

After the Revolution Casasola was contracted by the government of President Obregón, and later of President Calles, to be head of photography for various offices: in the Entertainments Department of the Government Secretariat, in the Public Register of Property of the Federal District Department, and in the work of recording prisoners and detainees for the judicial archive of the Belén courts. At this time Casasola produced and collected hundreds of thousands of plates which were added to his already famous Archive.

For some time Casasola had harboured the idea of publishing a selection of these photographs as a pictorial chronicle. This proposal, in a combination of testimony, initiative and commercial flair, saved the pictures from the ephemeral status of press illustrations and preserved them for posterity. In 1921 he began publication of the 'Album histórico gráfico', which ran from the last stages of the Díaz dictatorship up to the presidency of Alvaro Obregón. As new volumes appeared, they were expanded to include each new regime. This project was continued by his son Gustavo and ended with the 'Historia gráfica de la Revolución Mexicana' (ten volumes from the last decade of the Díaz dictatorship to the presidency of Echeverría), and the 'Seis siglos de historia gráfica de Mexico'. These two works make up the most ambitious and exhaustive editorial undertaking in Mexican photography. The old ballads were known under the name of the minstrel or troubadour who collected them. This great collective work continues the tradition, and is known under the name of the founders of the Archive, although we know that the work in it was produced by many photographers, some of them unknown. Yet in spite of the anonymity of many of its contributors, the era and the genres to which these works belong confer a special unity to the whole collection.

The Casasola albums are important in that they provide an exhaustive reference, although they illustrate only a part of what the Archive contains. But this is marred by the way in which the collectors laid out the pictures as well as by the weakness of the accompanying text. The selection, printing and layout of the images show an appalling neglect of the formal qualities of photography (a legacy perhaps of newsroom days) in favour of a desire to build up an historical chronology from the available fragments. With an anachronistic attachment to journalistic anecdote they give us a broken narrative illustrated with an abundance of grey images which impede our understanding of the events shown and our appreciation of the photographs.

Moreover, those interests which led the Casasolas to include certain pictures (mainly those showing revolutionary leaders, camp followers, pulqué drinkers and the rural life of the people) also intervened to eliminate others which were never published in the albums. Amongst these are many extraordinary images which, from a contemporary point of view, make an even more convincing case for the importance of Casasola in the history of photography.

The Casasolas never took a studio portrait, but they were outstanding portraitists. They succeeded in obtaining expressive pictures of individuals and groups in their usual environment (the factory, the prison, the market), in which the behaviour and attitude of the subject is completely natural. Casasola, as Posada and Orozco did in their own way, produced a gallery of characters of his time, all the more striking since they were captured within their social context. His training as a reporter developed in him a special sensitivity for that part of life which takes place in the community: on the street, at work, in politics, in the city.

By the very nature of the profession the reporter is often found in unusual situations — indeed he or she searches them out. The images which result are often seen from disconcerting angles and are far from routine. In this way the photographer can avoid the 'professional' distance with its moralising rhetoric and accusatory images which the editor demands, in order to capture moving scenes of desolation, grief and social distress. This sense of unease can be seen in photos of the detainees and prisoners at the Belén Prison taken at the end of the 1920s and beginning of the 1930s. The accused, subjected to the double interrogation of the judge and the lens, does not change expression in front of the camera, either evading it with a glance or confronting it impotently. The photographer behind the camera is not in the same position. He or she has to confront the accused in an environment which has nothing to do with festive, artificial and flattering studio props, but is in the midst of real and oppressive elements: the police, the judges, the prison warders, the lawyers. The photographer's vision becomes very uneasy when the discrimination of justice places before the lens children, women and working-class families who can only with a great effort of imagination be considered as criminal or guilty.

These photographs would undoubtedly have aroused much interest among contemporary photographers and avant-garde artists if they had had the opportunity to see them. Without conscious intention, Casasola was making photographs which in the richness of their expression transcended a simple in formative record. Casasola never set out to liberate photography from the influence of painting, or even to explore the formal possibilities inherent in the medium itself, nor much less to produce a committed body of work which reflected the conditions of life of the people under capitalism.

Such ideas were completely foreign to his mentality and his inclinations. Instead, almost unconsciously he succeeded in producing pictures which provided an inspiration to those artists of his time who worked with such ideas. An immense political distance would have made it impossible for Casasola to have any overt sympathy with the social orientation of the new photography and painting of the 1920s and 1930s. Nevertheless, we cannot help but ask ourselves what effect his work might have had on such artists as Tina Modotti and David Siqueiros if it had not remained obscure and mislaid for half a century in the vaults of the family Archive.

The history of Mexican photography is only now beginning to be written and Casasola's work cannot yet be placed precisely within any coherent development. The nearest obvious analogies, both in their subject matter and chronologically, are the work of the North American documentarist Lewis H. Hine — born in the same year as Casasola and died two years after him — and of some of the photographers, such as Dorothea Lange, who worked on the Farm Security Administration project, promoted by the US government in documenting the conditions in the rural areas most affected by the Depression. The similarity between the work of such photographers and the documentary photographs collected by Casasola is often striking. It arises not from direct influence (there is no evidence that they had ever seen each other's work), but from the similarity of conditions which brought the work about, in which times of crisis accentuate the negative effects of capitalism.

Casasola's contribution to the history of photography can no longer be ignored. His work loses nothing by being released from the myth of being revolutionary and from the ideological and commercial ballast which has kept it buried for so long. On the contrary, it now takes on its true value as a visual chronicle, as rich as that of which Agustín Víctor dreamed, and which is found not only in the pictures published by the family, but in the many other previously unpublished photographs which are only today beginning to be known.

Flora Lara Klahr
INAH Fototeca

★ Agustín Víctor Casasola. 'Historia gráfica de la Revolución Mexicana'. 2nd edition, volume 11, page 408. Mexico: Editorial Trillas, 1973.

The Photography of Revolution

'I love the Revolution as I love an erupting volcano! I love the volcano just because it is a volcano, and the Revolution because it is the Revolution! . . . But after the cataclysm who cares which stones are left on top and which underneath?'

Such were the passionate and fatalistic words of one of the characters in Mariano Azuela's revolutionary novel 'Los de abajo' ('The Underdogs'), written in 1915 at the height of the Civil War. Acceptance, perhaps, is a natural palliative for continued hardship. After five years of government and counter-government, of war and pillage in city and country, of torture and reprisals with no end in sight, the energy of destruction could seem seductive in itself; in this way a prisoner ceases to hate and learns to love his captor after years of incarceration. The prospect of cataclysm must, indeed, have seemed particularly attractive if it would cleanse the country of the old forms to make way for a new and humane Mexico. Similar dreams attracted many European intellectuals who, at the same time, enthusiastically supported the barbarism of the Great War.

Azuela was the first Mexican novelist to reflect contemporary reality in a fragmentary and unconnected way, depicting events and social types. He is concerned with the dynamism, rhythm and texture of society; causes and motivation remain intentionally unfocused.

The photographs of the Casasola Archive hold up a similar mirror to the face of Mexico; they reflect but do not comment. The work was commissioned by newspapers or government agencies and resulted from the labours of an army of staff and freelance photographers marshalled together by Agustín Víctor Casasola. It does not express any one vision or voice. Although many of the photographs were taken in prisons, orphanages and hospitals, and show an evident human sympathy, they cannot be thought of as 'committed' to any programme of social improvement in the way that Lewis Hine's or Jacob Riis's contemporary shots of New York slums so evidently are. The New York photographers were crusading intellectuals prepared to use their photographs as propaganda; those in Mexico were salaried employees.

The events of the Mexican Revolution were protracted, confused and bloody, but by the early 1920s the fabric of Mexican society had been fundamentally transformed. Naked power no longer rested with a small clique of landowners, willingly bolstered by the church and army, but had been transferred to an effective state bureaucracy which was starting to enforce the liberal political and social programmes of the Constitution of 1917.

The causes of the Revolution were rooted in the policies of President Porfirio Díaz; the atrocities of his long second term of office (1884-1911) matched many of the inhumanities of the Revolution. Díaz had consolidated his authority throughout the country with the help of powerful local political bosses ('haciendados') whom he rewarded for their services by the appropriation of peasants' lands. Industrialisation and modernisation had been achieved only at the cost of foreign investors being given a free hand. The resulting cynical exploitation of labour and raw materials mobilised public opinion against the foreign investors and identified Díaz and his circle as self seekers who cared little for the future of Mexico.

The opposition to Díaz centred around two issues: political reform and social reform. As early as 1906, from the safety of the United States, a call had been made for the return of the appropriated lands, the curbing of the power of the 'haciendados' and the restoration of press freedom. But it was on the specifically political issue of 'Effective Suffrage and No Re-Election' that popular support rallied around the candidacy of Francisco Madero in the 1910 presidential election — even though many of his supporters obviously hoped that this would bring social reform in its wake. The breadth of popular feeling for Madero panicked Díaz into imprisoning him on the eve of the election. This led to widespread riots, brutally suppressed by Díaz's 'Rurales' and triggered the successful military actions of Pascual Orozco and Francisco (Pancho) Villa in the north which led ultimately to Díaz's resignation and exile.

These events are well documented in the Casasola Archive. The photography of Díaz and his associates is formal and imposing; there is no indication of the social ferment under the surface. By the time that Casasola's cameramen had begun to respond to these changes, events had already begun to move swiftly: by April 1910 the main streets of the capital were crowded with mass demonstrations in favour of Madero. There was an elation and new sense of freedom, particularly evident in the series of photographs taken in Cuernavaca in 1911 when Madero was rapturously greeted by Emiliano Zapata and his 'peon' army. The elation was short-lived. Unrealistically, Madero thought that the Mexican people would be satisfied with political reform alone. He quickly lost the support of Zapata and his southern followers. In the north, Orozco also pressed for a programme of social reform and rebelled against the federal forces. Profiting from this dissension, the old regime staged a counter-attack led by Díaz's nephew, Félix, and Bernardo Reyes, a cabinet minister under the 'porfirista'. Hopelessly out of his political depth, Madero only managed to cling onto office through the effective, if ruthless, support of General Victoriano Huerta who controlled the army of the north.

There are a number of good photographs of Huerta's and Villa's campaign against Orozco and 'los colorados', as his rebel army was called. A vivid eye-witness account is given in English by John Reed, who spent the winter of 1913-14 with Villa's troops as war correspondent for 'Metropolitan' magazine. It is clear from these photographs that both generals were working soldiers who liked to involve themselves in the thick of combat. Villa, called a 'Mexican Robin Hood' by Reed, had attained notoriety as a bandit during the 'porfirista' following the murder of a government official. Now he unquestioningly and loyally supported Madero even after being imprisoned by him under the orders of Huerta; after the President's death in 1913 he openly wept at his grave.

Huerta, the blackguard of the Revolution, had turned against Villa and had ordered him to be shot as he could see in him a dangerous rival. This sentence was commuted to imprisonment by one of Madero's staff and after a few months in jail in Mexico City, Villa was allowed to escape. In February 1913 Huerta again showed his true colours. In the middle of Díaz's and Reyes's counter-coup in the capital, he cynically exploited the ten days of civil unrest and widespread killing (the 'Decena Trágica') to withdraw support from Madero to seize the presidency for himself. Madero was imprisoned and shot while trying to escape. Ruthless, perpetually intoxicated and administratively inept, Huerta maintained his shaky authority only through enforced conscription and a reign of terror.

All other factions combined against Huerta, but in October 1914 at the Convention of Aguascalientes, where all the revolutionary leaders met, Venustiano Carranza, head of the Constitutionalist forces, took the Maderist line that only political reform was necessary. Villa and Zapata held out for widespread social and land reform and took the initiative by occupying the capital. Eulalio Gutíerrez was installed as President. Carranza, with the support of the US

government, set up a provisional government in Veracruz.

The occupation of Mexico City is well documented: Villa, his murderous henchman Rodolfo Fierro, and Zapata ride with their troops down the Avenida San Francisco; they occupy the Presidential Palace and are photographed in the Presidential Chair. In spite of the surface camaraderie, both generals were deeply mistrustful of each other and unused to the ways of the city. Zapata in particular felt vulnerable to personal attack. To the cynical and ravaged inhabitants of the capital Zapata's indian followers must have seemed strange, uncomfortable and out of place. One photograph, in particular, captures this: a band of 'Zapatistas' has come to dine in the cafeteria of Sanborn's, one of the smartest department stores in the centre of the city.

Zapata soon returned to his homeland of Morelos in the south, but Villa engaged with Carranza's forces at Celaya in 1915. Prophetically, it was here that modern methods of warfare developed in Europe were first used in Mexico; General Obregón's carefully placed machine guns, barbed wire emplacements and trenches cut the impulsive Villista cavalry to shreds. Villa was never fully to recover from this total defeat.

The many photographs of Carranza, the new President, and Alvaro Obregón, his successor, have a stiffness and formality which is reminiscent of an earlier age. It was a time of stabilisation and the re-imposition of order. In 1917, at the Convention of Queretaro, Carranza had, under duress, approved the Constitution which is still in force today; the social concessions that it made were more radical than he would have liked and he showed little conviction in its enforcement. He began to resort to political assassination to maintain his power. After authorising the cowardly murder of Emiliano Zapata he, too, succumbed to the assassin's bullet. Order came at last with the presidency of Alvaro Obregón, whose Minister of Education, José Vasconcelos, modelled his far-sighted policies on those of Anatoly Lunacharsky, his Soviet counter-part. This stability was consolidated by Obregón's alliance with the urban workforce, for whom the issue of land reform was of little importance. Throughout the 1920s the government maintained a benevolent, if sometimes corrupting, hand on the rapidly growing power of the labour unions. The two worked together and, during the presidency of Elías Plutarco Calles, the Workers' Regional Confederation (CROM), with its boss Luis Morones, became the most influential labour organisation.

Besides those of the generals and leaders, there are many photographs of the common soldier, the innocent hero of the Revolution, usually taken at rest in encampments or in marshalling yards awaiting dispatch to the front. A number provide universal and unforgettable symbols of the melancholy and dislocation of war: the conscript, still wearing the bowler hat and dark suit he would have worn to the office, but now strung with a bandolier, looks out dolefully before boarding the train to join Huerta's army. In another picture, taken at about the same time, his country cousin, also waiting for orders, has pushed his sombrero down over his federal 'képi' and has wrapped his 'serape' around his backpack. The soldier has re-asserted his identity as a 'peon' — a man of the land.

Distances were so vast in this great war of skirmishes that soldiers had to support themselves off the land they occupied. In their campaigns they were joined by their women, the 'soldaderas', who in the many songs of the Revolution are as exalted as the generals. The 'soldadera' was the equal in courage and tenacity of her man. Orozco, the muralist, immortalised her on the walls of the National Preparatory School; Eisenstein took her image and dedicated a section of his unfinished film 'Qué Viva México'

to her. She appears frequently in the Casasola pictures; one in particular, often called 'Adelita' after the popular song, has become an icon of liberation.

Accounts of the Revolution, such as those of Azuela, José Clemente Orozco, John Reed and Martín Luis Guzmán, focus on such characters as typical of the pathos and heroism of the times. These symbols were also recognised by Casasola's photographers who, intuitively perhaps, provided a hagiography of the Revolution which has a universal as well as historical significance. These social types and symbols appearing in the popular illustrated press were the images through which many people perceived the Revolution. They subsequently provided a rich source of visual reference for the mural painters who, during the 1920s, began to paint the revolutionary history of Mexico.

In his urge to collect photographs it is clear that Casasola wanted to build up a pictorial reference of contemporary Mexico — an ambition no less grand in scale than that of August Sander, who, working in Germany at the same time, singlehandedly and systematically had begun his archive, 'Menschen des 20 Jahrhunderts' ('People of the 20th Century'). Sander, like Casasola, helped fund his project from commercial portraiture, advertising and industrial photography, yet his aims were more clear-cut. He wished to make a scientific visual record of different professions and physical types; within this plan a politician was no more important than a foundry worker. Casasola, as we have seen, had no such coherent plan, yet within the collection there is a gallery of professions and social types which, particularly in the later years, manifests the same brittle clarity as in Sander's portraits of the 1920s.

Within the Archive there are many facets. Yet another category of sensationalist photographs of murders, suicides and executions can be identified. In its clinical harshness and lack of compassion this work is perhaps closest in spirit to that of Arthur Fellig (Weegee) who worked with the New York Police Department during the 1930s and 1940s.

With such a large collection it is dangerous to generalise, but the view of Mexico that Casasola gives us after the Revolution reflects, as always, his location in the capital and the new modern spirit of the times. We see the music halls and burlesque shows, the rising unions and political demonstrations, but there is little indication of the lives of the peasants. These, perhaps, are Casasola's unsung heroes. In the far corners of the country, through their conviction suffering and dogged persistence, they held out for and eventually attained the cherished aims of the Revolution — their liberty and their land, paid for with their blood.

David Elliott

1884   Porfirio Díaz (1830-1915) began his second term as President. Under Díaz the presidency became like a dynasty and, in spite of constitutional controls, he remained in power until forcibly removed by the Revolution of 1910-17. In the early years of Díaz's rule Mexico experienced an unaccustomed political stability which encouraged economic growth. This was at a cost. Foreign investors rushed to exploit Mexico's ample raw materials. They were uncontrolled by the government and little thought was given to the country's economic or social welfare.

Díaz's social policies were formulated by a group of scientific, positivistic philosophers called 'los cientificos'. One of the most influential was José Limantour, Secretary of the Treasury.

1886   Guanajuato: the muralist Diego Rivera born (d. 1957).

1888   Railway line completed between Mexico City and Laredo, Texas — the shortest link to the USA. A time of economic expansion; by 1911 there were 15,000 miles of railway track within Mexico. Between 1874 and 1910 the population nearly doubled, to 15,160,000.

1900   Oil struck for the first time. Living standards for the majority of people did not improve, however. A twelve-hour working day was usual with no time off at weekends. Infant mortality averaged 30 per cent. Under Díaz, the rich ranch owners ('haciendados') began to appropriate common land and refused to let peasants or Indians farm it. The 'haciendado' became a great landowner and political chief. Land, power and wealth became concentrated in a few hands.

Oaxaca: the painter Rufino Tamayo born. Founding of 'Regeneracion', revolutionary journal of Ricardo Flores Magón. First published in Mexico City, later in San Antonio, Texas, St Louis and Los Angeles.

1904   Augustín Yañez born. Yañez was one of the pioneers of Mexico's 'new novel'.

1906   Strike of miners in Cananea, Sonora, brutally suppressed by the authorities. Reformist junta exiled in St Louis, USA, published 'The Liberal Plan'. It called for, among other things: freedom of speech and the press; suppression of political bosses; secularisation of education; restoration of appropriated lands. First attempt (September-October) of Flores Magón to launch rebellion in Chihuahua and Sonora.

1907   Strikes: Rio Blanco Textile Mills. Cruelly suppressed.

1908   Diego Rivera to Spain to study painting. Travelled widely through northern Europe. Returned to Mexico 1910. Back in Paris 1911; stayed until 1920. Díaz said that he would not seek re-election at the end of his term of office in two years' time. Opposition to his regime centred on the slogan 'No Re-election'. Publication in 'Pearson's Magazine' of James Creelman's interview with Porfirio Díaz in which Díaz said he would welcome formation of opposition party. Second attempt of 'Magonistas' to launch a revolution; Liberal Party members arrested throughout Mexico. Francisco I. Madero finishes writing 'The Presidential Succession in 1910', but does not distribute it until following year.

1909   Publication of 'Great National Problems' by Andrés Molina Enríquez, a thorough study of the land question.

1910   Halley's Comet interpreted as evil omen. Celebration of centennial of war of independence. Francisco Madero, a liberal, emerged as leader of the Anti-Re-electionists. He believed in political rather than social reform: 'The Mexican people do not want bread. They want liberty.' Madero imprisoned by Díaz on eve of election. Díaz's 'victory' proclaimed. On release from jail Madero published 'The Plan of San Luis Potosí', declaring the election illegal and calling

for mass civil uprisings on 20 November.
20 Nov: many peasant uprisings. They were largely suppressed by Díaz's efficient paramilitary police, the 'Rurales', except in the north in Chihuahua. There, rebel Pascual Orozco gathered a large army which included the bandit Francisco (Pancho) Villa. They waged a successful campaign against government troops.

1911   May: rebels won battle of Cuidad Juárez. Díaz resigned the presidency.
Oct: Madero elected President. Díaz: 'Madero has unleashed a Tiger. Now let's see if he can control it.' Emiliano Zapata (1879-1919), rebel leader in the south, asked Madero to restore the appropriated lands immediately. Madero would not agree.
Nov: Zapata issued 'The Plan of Ayala'. This withdrew recognition of Madero as President and asked that: 'the lands, woods and water that the landlords, cientificos, and bosses have usurped . . . will be immediately restored'.

1912   March: 'The Plan Orozquista'; Pascual Orozco withdrew his support from Madero and re-iterated the demands of 'The Liberal Plan' of 1906. Orozco marched on Mexico City but was stopped by the troops of General Victoriano Huerta. Félix Díaz, nephew of the former dictator, staged a revolt with General Bernardo Reyes. This was suppressed and both were imprisoned.

1912-13   Manuel Ponce called for a new national music; composed his 'canciones mexicanas'.

1913   From prison Reyes and Díaz staged a coup. They escaped and for ten days Mexico City was in the grips of a violent and destructive civil war, the 'Decena Trágica'. Madero asked Huerta to fight on his behalf but after nine days of vicious combat, and under strong pressure from the US Ambassador, Huerta changed sides. Madero was defeated, arrested and shortly afterwards murdered. Huerta was made President. This regime was not recognised by the troops in the north, however. Venustiano Carranza, Governor of Coahuila and ardent supporter of Madero, refused to recognise Huerta. He gained support from Pancho Villa in Chihuahua and Alvaro Obregón in Sonora.
March: These three signed 'The Plan of Guadalupe'. Carranza was recognised as First Chief of the Constitutional Army. In the south, Zapata also refused to recognise Huerta as he saw no hope for the restoration of land to the peasants. Both sides inflicted serious losses on Huerta. He became increasingly dictatorial and relied on political assassination to stay in power. Villa had a series of victories at Torreon, Juárez, Tierra Blanca and Ojinaga.

1914   The writer Octavio Paz born in Mexico City. The USA refused to recognise Huerta's presidency. After a minor diplomatic incident between the US Navy and Huerta's government in Tampico, President Woodrow Wilson ordered his navy to occupy Veracruz.
July: Huerta resigned the presidency.
Oct: 'The Convention of Aguascalientes' called by Carranza to decide on a provisional President. Zapata's representative under the slogan 'Effective suffrage and no re-election' recognised only Villa and Zapata as the true leaders of the Revolution. Serious rift developed between Carranza's supporters, who favoured politically oriented solutions, and Villa and Zapata's supporters, who wished to adopt the agrarian reforms of 'The Plan of Ayala'. No agreement was reached.
Eulalio Gutiérrez elected President but not recognised by Carranza, who then withdrew to Veracruz. The US troops turned the city over to him as provisional capital. Anarchy followed and many atrocities were committed on all sides. USA lifted arms embargo, thus aiding rebels. Carranza left Sonora for Chihuahua; beginning of his rift with Villa. Villa as head of Conventionist forces retook Torreon. Villa's victory at Zacatecas and Obregón's at Guadalajara sealed fate of Huerta's army. Obregón took control of Mexico City.

Carranza assumed the title of First Chief in charge of executive power; summoned a junta of generals and governors to plan future. Carranza fled Mexico City, making Veracruz — recently evacuated by US troops — his capital. Obregón in command of Carranza's forces. Villa and Zapata control Mexico City.

1915   Mariano Azuela (1873-1952) published 'Los de abajo' ('The Underdogs'), a classic Mexican social novel.
April: Battle of Celaya. Villa attacked Carranzist forced led by Obregón and was routed. Based on Europe's example, barbed wire and machine guns effectively used against Villa's cavalry for the first time.
Oct: USA officially recognised Carranza's regime. Villa isolated in the north; turned his attention to raiding US border towns. Carranza acknowledged need for land reform, issued moderate agrarian decree. Eulalio Gutiérrez, unable to control Villa, fled Mexico City. Obregón took Puebla, then Mexico City, then defeated Villa in battle at Celaya. Villa suffered further defeats at León, Aguascalientes, Zacatecas, Agua Prieta, Hermosillo, and by end of year was no longer a major military force. Convention government dissolved. Carranza, claiming control of seven-eighths of Mexico, recognised on *de facto* basis by USA.

1916   March: Villa attacked Colombus, New Mexico, killing 18 US citizens. President Wilson authorised punitive expedition to pursue Villa into Mexico led by General J.J. (Black Jack) Pershing. Carranza immediately asked Pershing to withdraw but he refused. The US force stayed on Mexican soil until January 1917.
Nov: Carranza called convention of Constitutionalists in Queretaro.

1917   Convention continued into 1917, resulting in the foundation of the Constitution which is still in force today. It was more radical than Carranza would have liked: free and obligatory primary education; restitution of appropriated lands; only Mexican nationals to exploit natural resources; power of the Church restricted; 8-hour workday, 6-day week; equal pay for work regardless of sex or nationality.
May: Carranza elected President. Chaos — few of the articles of the new Constitution implemented. Carranza moved against Zapata in Morelos. German foreign minister's efforts to enlist Mexico on Germany's side caused international scandal. Carranza remained neutral.

1919   April: Zapata lured to a meeting with one of Carranza's agents and murdered. Death of Amado Nervo, one of the most important modernist writers. His analysis of psychological problems was strongly influenced by the French realists, particularly Flaubert. Ambassador Ignacio Bornillas chosen by Carranza as his successor. Obregón announced his candidacy, and had difficulty campaigning.

1920   Obregón turned against Carranza and with a new northern army marched on Mexico City. Carranza fled, deserted by most of his followers, and assassinated on his way to exile. Obregón elected President. The Revolution drew to an end. Between 1.5 and 2 million people had been killed in ten years of civil war. Obregón created a portfolio for education. Gave post to José Vasconcelos, who immediately started to provide basic educational facilities throughout Mexico. During 1920-24 over 1,000 rural schools built and 2,000 public libraries established. Vasconcelos was also responsible for commissioning the murals at the National Preparatory School in 1923. Orozco, Rivera, Siqueiros and others were approached.
Under interim presidency of Adolfo de la Huerta there was a period of reconciliation among revolutionary factions: Villa accepted amnesty, retired to Canutillo.

1922   Secretary of the Treasury de la Huerta went to New York; Lamont Agreement negotiated regarding Mexican debts.

1923   Rivera started murals in the Ministry of

Public Education, Mexico City. These were completed by 1928. Pancho Villa murdered. Revolution against Obregón by conservatives, the military and nationalists, led by Adolfo de la Huerta. The uprising was short but violent; over 7,000 were killed. Obregón recognised by USA after completion of Bucareli pact on debts, land expropriation and oil. De la Huerta, supported by conservatives and much of the army, rebelled against the government. Shortly afterwards went into exile.

1924 Jan: Governor of Yucatan and champion of peasants Felipe Carillo Puerto assassinated. Puerto was enaged to be married to Alma Reed, Orozco's biographer. Obregón peacefully handed over the presidency to Plutarco Calles.

1924-34 Calles stayed in power for the next ten years. Started with liberal intentions but became increasingly dictatorial. Political prisoners proliferated as did political assassinations. Worked closely with Luis Morones and CROM, the leading labour organisation; Morones made Secretary of Labour.

1925 Philosopher Antonio Caso published 'Principles de estetica', an influential book stating that morality had to be based on sacrifice and love. Manuel Alverez Bravo made first photographic work. Publication of José Vasconcelos's 'La raza cosmica', emphasising the positive virtue of Indian ways. Calles supported schismatic Mexican Catholic Apostolic church.

1925-30 Siqueiros abandoned painting to work politically with radical trade unions.

1926-27 Rivera worked on murals at Chapingo, then visited the Soviet Union. Calles issued anti-Catholic decrees; in retaliation Catholics suspended church services throughout Mexico.

1926-28 The Cristero Rebellion. Catholic uprising against the anti-clerical enforcements of the Calles government. Obregón to run for President again; his supporters amend Constitution to permit re-election, also extending presidential term from four to six years. Presidential aspirants Francisco Serrano and Arnulfo Gomez and their followers are executed. Four men accused of bomb attempt on Obregón's life executed without trial, among them Miguel Pro, a Jesuit priest active in the Catholic underground. Dwight Morrow, new US Ambassador, exercising strong influence on Calles.

1928 Election: Obregón won, but assassinated before assuming office. Novelist Carlos Fuentes born, Mexico City. Emilio Portes Gil named provisional President; Calles out of office, retaining great influence as 'Jefe Maximo'. Formation of 'Partido Nacional Revolucionario' (PNR).

1929 Election: won by Calles as 'eminence grise' behind Pasceul Ortiz Rubio, the head of the PNR. Vasconcelos fought in election but defeated. Martín Luis Guzmán published novel 'La sombra del caudillo', a passionate condemnation of dictatorship and corruption. Calles, increasingly conservative, declared both agrarianism and the Revolution to be failures.

1929-34 A time of increasing political control and repression in Mexican society. Support of CROM was dropped. More money spent on armed forces. 1930-31 anti-communist hysteria. Formation of the fascist organisation the Gold Shirts. Rivera started mural on main staircase of National Palace; also named Director of Academy of San Carlos. Painted mural in Palace of Cortez, Cuernavaca.

1930 Attempt on life of Ortiz Rubio on his inauguration day. Bodies of more than 100 followers of Vasconcelos, all strangled, found in shallow graves at Topilejo.

1931 Siqueiros imprisoned for political activity.

1932 Russian film director Sergei Eisenstein in Mexico filming 'Qué Viva México'. Ortiz Rubio, discouraged by interference of Calles in his administration, resigned and left Mexico. Abelardo Rodriguez, a businessman-general,

appointed to complete the term.

1934 Lazaro Cardenas elected President. Film: Ezequiel Carrasco's 'Viva Mexico!' Mexican film industry developing. PNR adopted Six Year Plan as a programme of government.

1935 Carlos Chavez (1899-1978) composed 'Symphonia India' and 'Oberatura Republicana'. Chavez studied the music of the Indian and incorporated their rhythms and melodies into his work. Cardenas, elected as a puppet of Calles, quickly began to establish his independence. Aimed to revitalise the Revolution and carry it further to the left. He removed all Calles's supporters from the cabinet; in 1936 Calles himself arrested and exiled. The agrarian reform programme was pushed forward and some 49 million acres of land given back to the communities which had originally owned them. More money was spent on education and health particularly in rural areas. Considerable successes were offset, though, by a very large rise in the population. Organised labour was strengthened. Vicente Lombardo Toledano took the place of the discredited Luis Morones as the head of the Confederation de Trabajadores de Mexico (CTM).

Pancho Villa

Selected Bibliography

Azuela, Mariano (trans. E. Munguia). 'The Underdogs'. New York: New American Library, 1963.

Berdecio, Roberto, and Appelbaum, Stanley, eds. 'Posada's Popular Mexican Prints'. New York: Dover Publications, 1972.

Brenner, Anita, 'Idols behind Altars: The Story of the Mexican Spirit'. Boston: Beacon Press, 1970.

Brenner, Anita, and Leighton, George. 'The Wind that Swept Mexico: The History of the Mexican Revolution 1910-1942'. Austin: University of Texas Press, 1971.

Brushwood, John S. 'Mexico in Its Novel: A Nation's Search for Identity'. Austin: University of Texas Press, 1966.

Calvert, Peter. 'Mexico. Nation of the Modern World'. London: Ernest Benn, 1973.

Casasola, Gustavo, ed. 'Historia gráfica de la Revolución Mexicana 1900-1960' (10 volumes). Mexico: Editorial Gustavo Casasola, 1964.

Casasola, Gustavo, ed. 'Seis siglos de historia gráfica de Mexico 1325-1970' (7 volumes). Mexico: Editorial Gustavo Casasola, 5th edition, 1976.

Charlot, Jean. 'The Mexican Mural Renaissance, 1920-1925'. New Haven: Yale University Press, 1967.

Guzmán, Martín Luis (trans. Harriet de Onís). 'The Eagle and the Serpent'. Gloucester: Peter Smith, 1969.

Meyer, Michael C., and Sherman, William L. 'The Course of Mexican History' (2nd edition). New York: Oxford University Press, 1983.

Mora, Carl J. 'Mexican Cinema. Reflections of a Society 1896-1980'. Berkeley: University of California Press, 1982.

Orozco, José Clemente (trans. Robert C. Stephenson). 'An Autobiography'. Austin: University of Texas Press, 1962.

Reed, Alma. 'Orozco'. New York: Oxford University Press, 1956.

Reed, John. 'Insurgent Mexico'. London: Penguin, 1983.

Rutherford, John. 'Mexican Society during the Revolution. A Literary Approach'. London: Oxford University Press, 1971.

Simmons, Merle E. 'The Mexican Corrido as a Source for Interpretive Study of Modern Mexico (1870-1950)'. Bloomington: Indiana University Press, 1957.

Siqueiros, David Alfaro. 'Art and Revolution'. London: Lawrence & Wishart, 1975.

Sommers, Joseph. 'After the Storm'. Albuquerque: University of New Mexico Press, 1968.

Tyler, Ron, ed. 'Posada's Mexico'. Washington DC: Library of Congress, 1979.

Wolfe, Bertram D. 'The Fabulous Life of Diego Rivera'. New York: Stein & Day, 1969.

Zuver, Marc, ed. 'The World of Agustín Víctor Casasola. Mexico 1900-1938'. Washington DC: The Fondo del Sol Visual Art and Media Center, 1984.

¡TIERRA! ¡Y LIBERTAD!

Rendicion del Genl. Villa Casasola Fot. M.y.

Pancho Villa awaits the arrival of General Eugenio Martínez to finalise the details of de la Huerta's surrender. Coahuila. July 1920

THE PHOTOGRAPHS

Porfirio Díaz at a ceremony commemorating the death of President Benito Juárez. July 191

verleaf: Guillermo de Landa y Escandón, Governor of Mexico City, with his family. c. 1910

Officers of the federal army. c. 1900

English cyclist act. c. 1905

Textile mill. Mexico City. c. 1908. Overleaf: Exhibition of 'natives and poisonous animals.' Mexico City. 1905

Execution of Arcadio Jiménez, Hilario Silva and Marcelino Martínez, murderers of Tomás Morales. Chalco. 28 April 19

Above: Sara Pérez de Madero with her son
and Sra Mercedes González de Madero, mother
of the President, on a visit to a dress-making
workshop. Mexico City. 1912
Left: Francisco (Pancho) Villa weeping
at the grave of Francisco Madero. Mexico City.
8 Dec 1914
Opposite page: Francisco I. Madero with his
secretary signing peace treaty with the Díaz
government, after successful campaign by Villa.
Following this Díaz resigned the presidency
and free elections were called.
Ciudad Juárez, Chihuahua. 21 May 1911

MADERO
SU SECRETARIO
PATICULAR C. ILARES
CASASOLA FOT MEX

MARTES 23 DE ABRIL DE 1912.

28 **Revolutionary supporters of Madero. 23 April 1912**

Revolutionary supporters of Madero. c. 1911
Below: Madero, escorted by Emiliano Zapata and members of his army during presidential election campaign.
Cuernavaca, Morales. 12 June 1911
Opposite page: Felipe Angeles, general in charge of artillery in Villa's northern division. 1914

Pancho Villa and his pro-Madero troops before the successful attack on Ciudad Juárez. May 1911

GENERALES HUERTA
RABAGO Y
TELLE
DESPUES DE LA BATALLA DE
RELLANO

Gral. Francisco VILLA
EN EL EsTribo de su TREN
CASASOLA F.T. Mex

Pancho Villa is taken prisoner under the orders of General Victoriano Huerta. Mexico City. June 1912
Opposite page, top: Victoriano Huerta, Emilio Madero and Pancho Villa, leaders of the northern division of the federal army, after defeating General Pascual Orozco's rebellion at Conejos. May 1912
Below: Generals Huerta, Rábago and Telles after the battle of Rellano against Orozco. Coahuila. 24 May 1912

Above: Fleeing from the danger zone
during the 'Decena Trágica' — ten tragic days
during which Bernardo Reyes and
Félix Díaz, nephew of Don Porfirio,
escaped from prison and led a bloody uprising
against Madero. Mexico City. Feb 1913
Left: General Victoriano Huerta returns
to Mexico City after his successful campaign
against Orozco's rebels. Oct 1912
Overleaf: During the 'Decena Trágica',
Huerta withdrew his support from Madero and
seized the presidency himself.
his formal portrait with his General Staff
was taken in the National
Palace soon after that time. 1913

Federal 'rurales' dispatch teams of horses to
troops fighting the Constitutionalists.
Buenavista Station, Mexico City. 18 May 1914
Overleaf: 'Soldaderas' with the federal troops. 1911-14

Federal soldiers waiting to leave for La Laguna to fight against Constitutionalist revolutionaries. Mexico City. March-April 1913

50 **Encampment of federal troops at Ixtlán, Oaxaca. 1913**

Federal conscripts. Mexico City. c. 1915
Right: Boy soldier for the federal army. Mexico City. c. 1915
Overleaf: Federal troops and volunteers gather prior to dispatch to the front.
Mexico City. April 1913

Delegates at the Convention of Aguascalientes. Teatro Morelos. Oct 1914
Opposite page: After defeating Victoriano Huerta, Venustiano Carranza, First Chief of the Constitutionalist army, occupies the National Palace. Mexico City. 20 Aug 1914
Overleaf: Colonel Alfonso Aguilar, deserter from the Constitutionalist army, bids farewell to his friends. Mexico City. Feb 1916

Above: Villa and Zapata, with Tomás Urbina and Rodolfo Fierro, head the combined troops of the northern division and the army of the south as they march into Mexico City. 6 Dec 1914
Far left: Villa, Zapata and their followers in the Presidential Room of the National Palace. Mexico City. 6 Dec 1914
Centre: José Vasconcelos, Villa, President Eulalio Gutiérrez and Zapata at a celebratory banquet in the National Palace. Mexico City. Dec 1914
Left: President Eulalio Gutiérrez with Eufemio Zapata, Emiliano's brother, and others in the National Palace. Mexico City. 4 Dec 1914
Overleaf: Waitresses at Sanborn's department store serving breakfast to Zapata's followers. Mexico City. Dec 1914

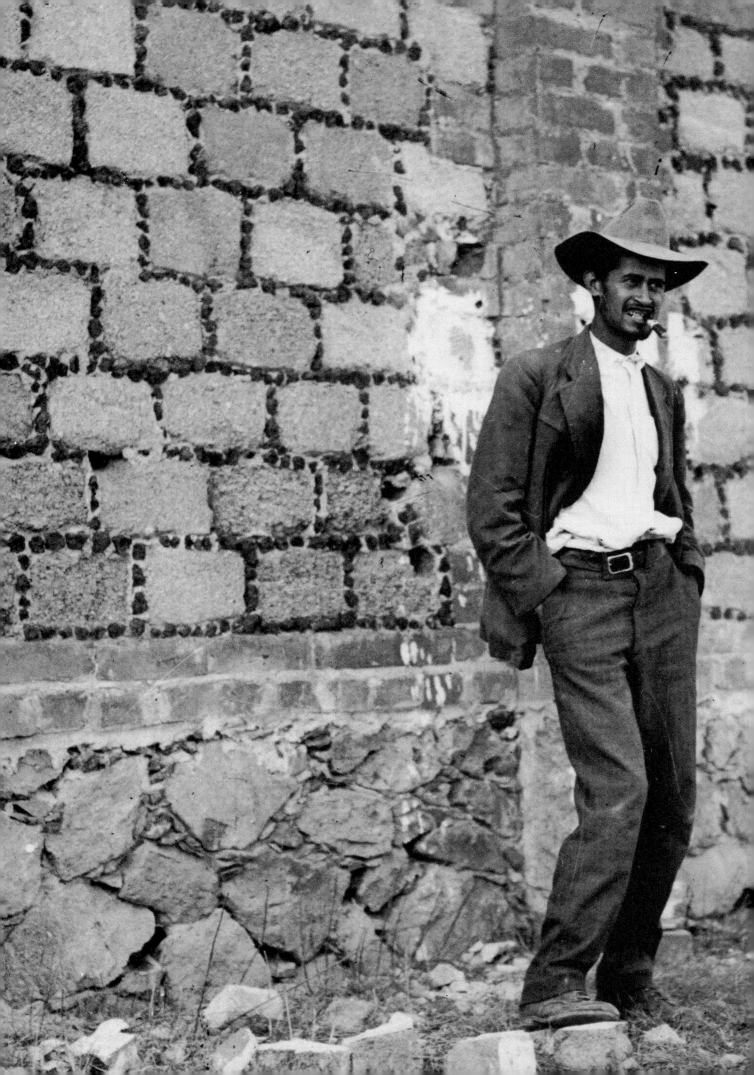

Captain Fortino Sámano smokes
a last cigar before execution
by the Constitutionalist authorities
for crimes of theft, violence and
other misdemeanours. 12 Jan 1917

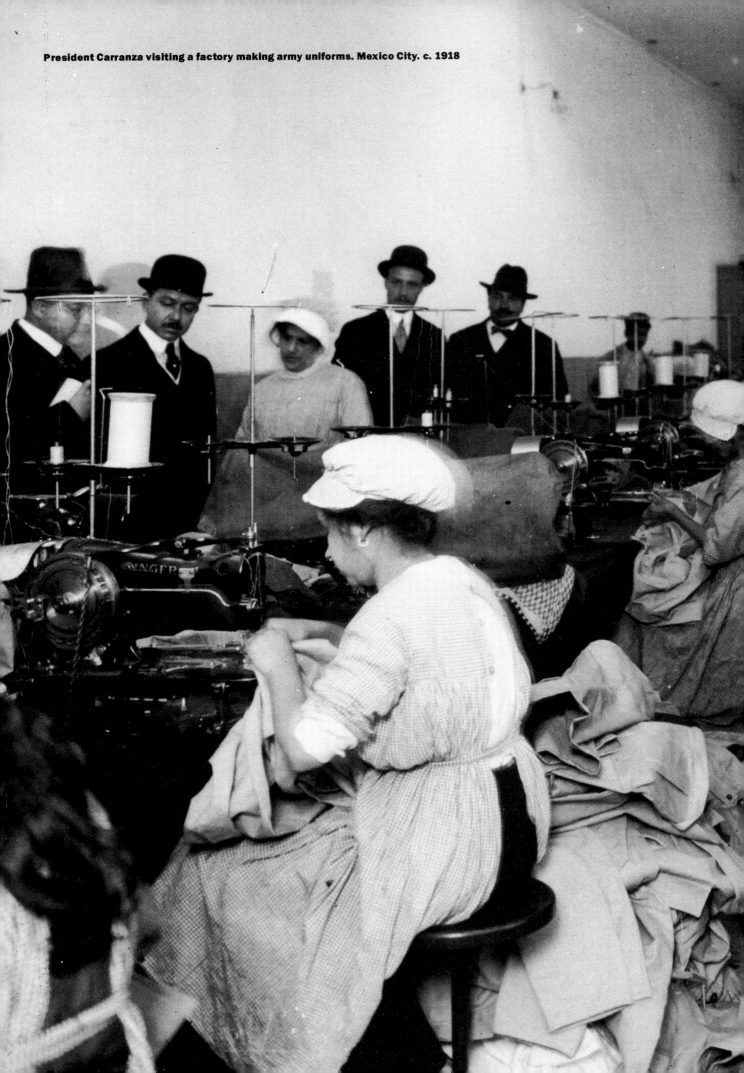

President Carranza visiting a factory making army uniforms. Mexico City. c. 1918

Emiliano Zapata assassinated by the agents of Carranza. Cuatla, Morales. 10 April 1919

President Carranza assassinated by a member of his own bodyguard. Tlaxcalantongo, Puebla. May 1920

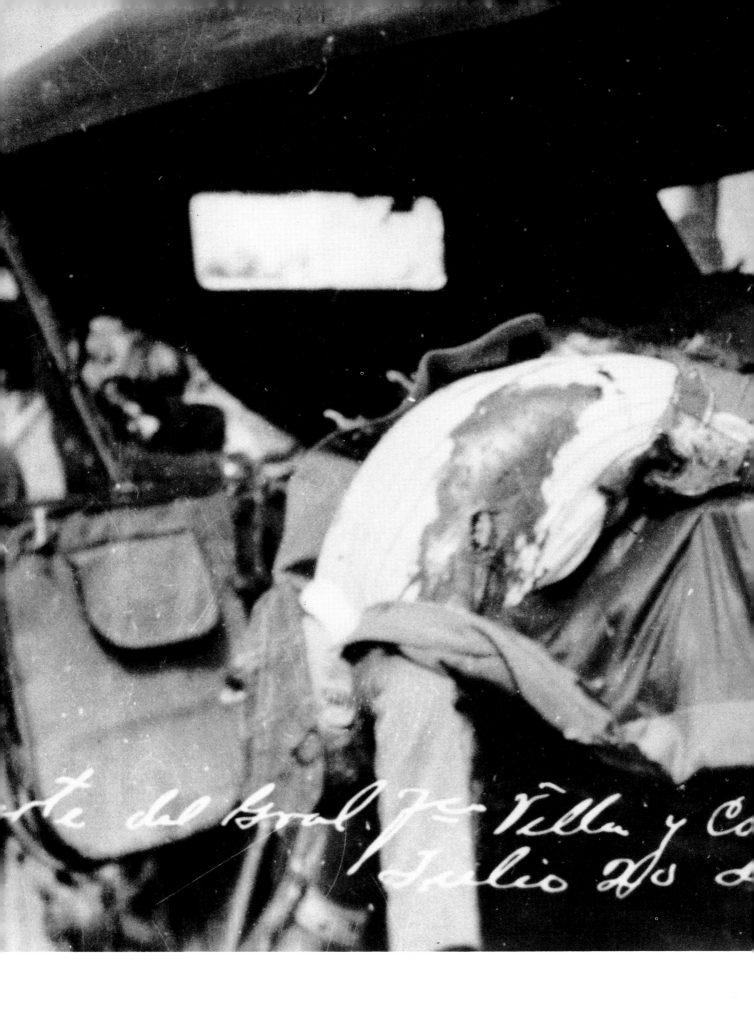

Previous page: General Pilar Sánches, Heliodoro Perez and others, escorts of President Carranza at the time of his death, are taken prisone Beristain, Puebla. May 1920

General Miguel Trillo in the car in which he was murdered along with Pancho Villa. Parral, Chihuahua. 20 July 1923

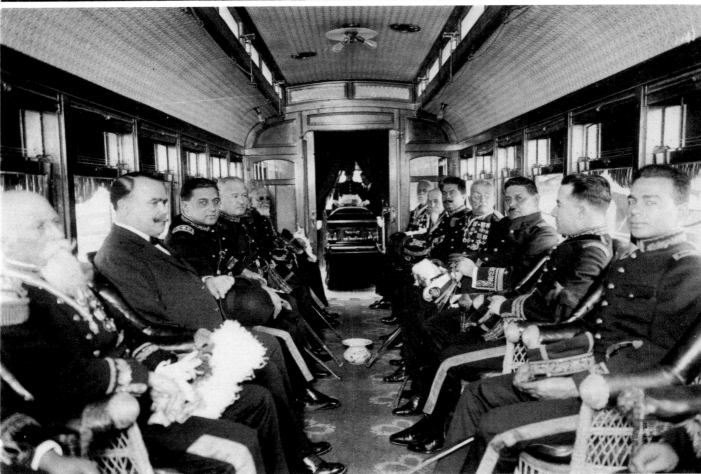

President Alvaro Obregón with members of the diplomatic corps and war veterans. Mexico City. c. 1922
Top: President Obregón and guests at a ball in the Chapultepec Restaurant. Mexico City. Oct 1921
Opposite page: President Obregón (2nd row, right), José Vasconcelos (3rd row, left), Plutarco Elías Calles (1st row, 2nd from left),
Fernando Torreblanca (3rd row, right) and other officials. Mexico City. c. 1923

**North American acrobats,
Circo Orrín. Mexico City. 1901
Right: Singers, Mexico City. 1925**

North American chorus girls making their successful debut in Mexico City. c. 1925
Below: World Champions of Graeco-Roman wrestling. Mexico City. 1925. Opposite page: Dancer in Vaudeville show. Mexico City. c. 1925
Overleaf: Newspaper boys. Mexico City. c. 1914

Workers in 'El Buen Tono' tobacco factory. Mexico City. c. 1905
Opposite page: Workers in the Condesa boiler works. Mexico City. c. 1930
Overleaf: Railway workers. Mexico City. c. 1940

Cleaners and transport workers affiliated to CROM (the Mexican Workers' Regional Confederation). Mexico City. 1922

Above and overleaf: Funeral procession for Florentino Ramos who died during a confrontation between workers and management in the textile mills of San Angel. Mexico City. 25 Oct 1922
Right: Diego Rivera leads funeral procession of Julio Antonio Mella, the Cuban revolutionary and companion of Tina Modotti, who was assassinated in Mexico City. 10 Jan 1929
Far right: David Alfaro Siqueiros and others preside over a memorial gathering in honour of Julio Antonio Mella.

Mexico City. 1931-32

Sentence. Mexico City. c. 1928

Prisoner at Belén. Mexico City. c. 1928

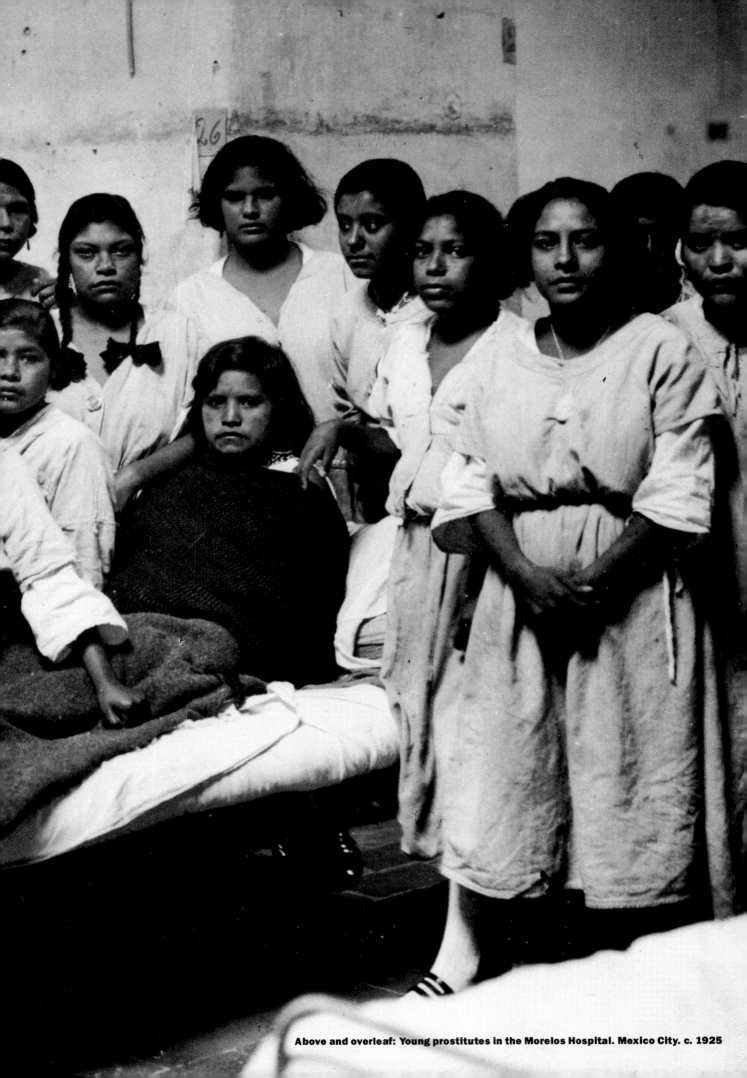

Above and overleaf: Young prostitutes in the Morelos Hospital. Mexico City. c. 1925

Tlalpan prison. Mexico City. c. 1918
Below: Newspaperboys. Mexico City. c. 1920
Opposite page: Alvaro and Mayo, sons of General Obregón. Mexico City. Early 1920s

Belén prison. Mexico City. c. 1927

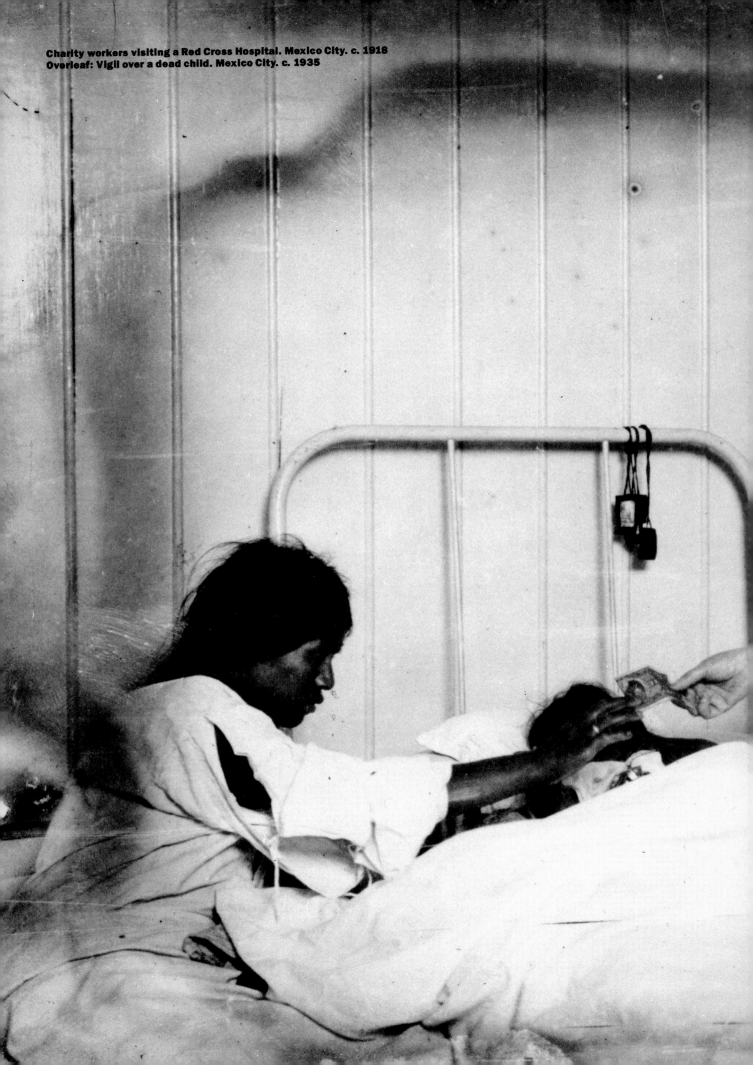

Charity workers visiting a Red Cross Hospital. Mexico City. c. 1918
Overleaf: Vigil over a dead child. Mexico City. c. 1935

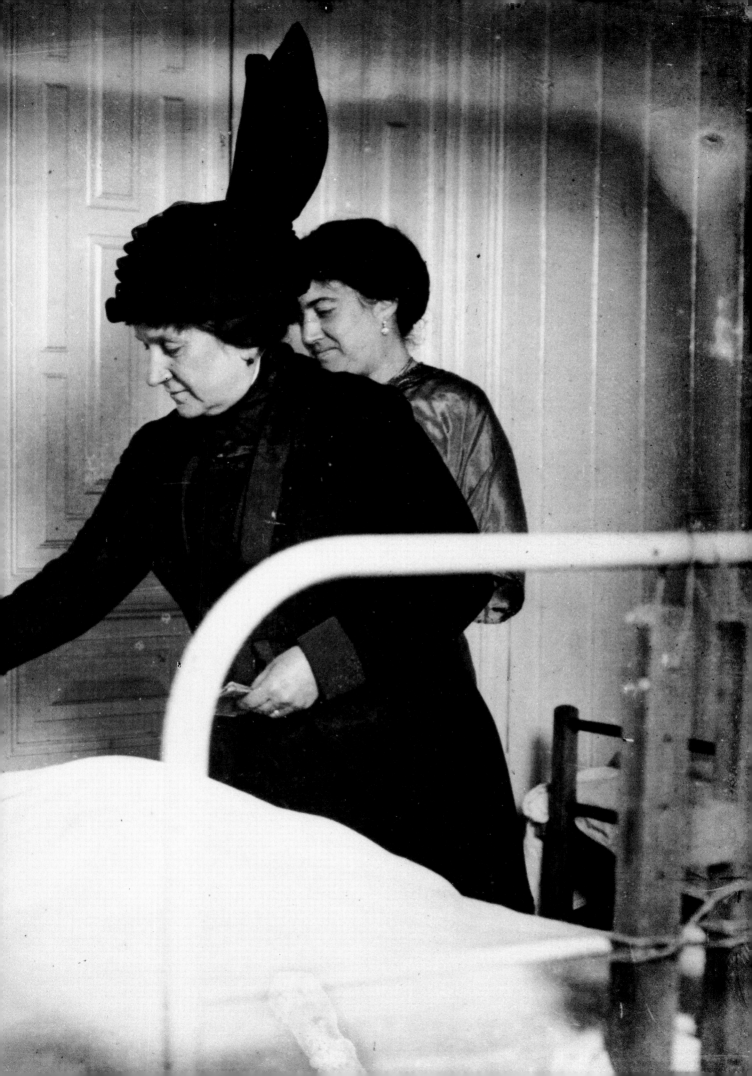